To-
Sid Sperry
– best wish
John

Sid –
Have a wonderful
holiday season!
Parry Alleghery
12-25-97

Sid,
Wishing you
and your family
a joyous and happy
Holiday Season
Pat Shore

THIRTEEN DAYS OF TERROR

THIRTEEN DAYS OF TERROR

The Rufus Buck Gang in Indian Territory

BY GLENN SHIRLEY

Barbed Wire Press
PO Box 2107, Stillwater, OK 74076
A Western Publications Company

Library of Congress Cataloging-in-Publication Data

Shirley, Glenn.
  Thirteen Days of Terror: The Rufus Buck Gang in Indian
  Territory / by Glenn Shirley.– 1st. Edition
  p. cm.
  Includes biblographical references and index.
  ISBN 0-935269-22-3
  1. Buck, Rufus. 2. Outlaws–Indian Territory–Biougraphy
  3. Indian Territory–History–19th century. 4. Frontier and
   Pioneer life–Indian Territory. I. Title
  F698.B83S48 1996
  973.0497–dc20

Cover design by Marcus Huff
Copyright © 1996 by Glenn Shirley
All rights reserved.
Published by Barbed Wire Press, PO Box 2107, Stillwater, OK
   74076-2107. 800-749-3369.
Manufactured in the United States of America. First Edition.

CONTENTS

Preface	ix
Prologue	xiii
1. Rob! Kill! Rape Their Women!	3
2. Corporate Outlaws	10
3. Murder of Deputy Marshal John Garrett	18
4. "Criminality Without Parallel...."	23
5. Outrage on Snake Creek	32
6. Battle at Flat Rock	38
7. "Some of You Will Die!"	47
8. A Flood of Evidence	56
9. Promised Justice Done	65
Notes	73
Bibliography	79
Index	83

ILLUSTRATIONS

Map of Indian Territory	xv
Map of the Creek Nation, about 1898	5
Samuel Morton Rutherford, United States Marshal	15
James B. McDonough, Assistant United States District Attorney	28
Muskogee *Phoenix,* August 8, 1895	40
Muskogee *Phoenix,* August 15, 1895	45
Creek Council House at Okmulgee	49
Rufus Buck Gang at Fort Smith	55
Judge Isaac Parker	63
The Fort Smith *Elevator,* July 3, 1896, and Muskogee *Phoenix*, July 9, 1896	66
Rufus Buck's "My Dream" (poem)	70

PREFACE

From 1894 to 1895, organized bands of renegades and fugitives from justice swept the nations of the Five Civilized Tribes and raided into the bordering states of Kansas, Texas, Missouri, and Arkansas. These were the waning years of Isaac Charles Parker's tenure as judge of the United States district and circuit courts for the Western District of Arkansas at Fort Smith, with jurisdiction over Indian Territory. Fortunately for civilization itself, most of those gangs were brought to bay in Judge Parker's court or stamped out by federal officers, Indian police, and citizens' posses.

The Daltons met disaster while robbing two banks at Coffeyville, Kansas, in 1892. The Henry Starr gang was broken up in 1893, and Starr himself languished in jail at Fort Smith pending an appeal to the United States Supreme Court after being twice sentenced to hang for the murder of a deputy United States marshal. The Nathaniel

"Texas Jack" Reed gang was shattered in a train robbery at Blackstone Switch, Creek Nation, in 1894. In March of 1895, the Bob Rogers train robbing bunch were shot to pieces at Horseshoe Mound, Cherokee Nation. The Bill Cook-Cherokee Bill marauders looted and killed for six months from mid-1894 before being brought to an inevitable end. Cook received a long term in a New York penitentiary. Cherokee Bill was awaiting execution for killing an innocent bystander during one of his robberies, and with an appeal pending in the United States Supreme Court, killed a guard while attempting a wholesale delivery of prisoners from the federal jail at Fort Smith. He would eventually die at rope's end on St. Patrick's Day, March 1896.

It was the Buck gang of ravishers, however, who provided the brutality and rapine for the most startling, if not the most dreadful, chapter of Indian Territory brigandage.

There were five of them: Rufus Buck, Luckey Davis, Sam Sampson, and Maomi July—all Creek full-bloods and half-bloods—and Lewis Davis, an African-American. Two-bit horse thieves and whiskey peddlers, individually, they sprang up as corporate outlaws in late July 1895 and flourished with complete abandon for thirteen days.

Considering the length of time this quintet operated, they made the Daltons, Starrs, Reeds, and the others look like pikers. Owing to the heinous nature of their crimes, they stand easily at the head of all the dissolute characters who were swung on the gallows at Fort Smith, and must go down as the meanest, dirtiest little band of outlaws in America.

GLENN SHIRLEY
Stillwater, Oklahoma

PROLOGUE

By the mid-1890s, present-day Oklahoma was known as the "Twin Territories." Oklahoma Territory, created by the Organic Act of May 2, 1890, consisted of the original six counties carved from the Unassigned Lands opened to settlement in 1889 and a seventh county called "Beaver" encompassing the panhandle ("No Man's Land"). It included the reservation of the Iowa, Sac and Fox, and Pottawatomie-Shawnee Indians, opened in 1891; the Cheyenne-Arapaho reservation, opened in 1892; the Cherokee Outlet ("Strip") west of the Arkansas River, opened in 1893, together with the Kaw, Tonkawa, Ponca, Otoe-Missouri, and Pawnee reservations therein; and the Kickapoo reservation, opened in 1895. The far southwestern reservations of the Wichita-Caddo and Kiowa-Comanche-Apache tribes (eventually opened by "drawings" and "sealed bids" in 1901 and 1906), and the Osage Nation east of the Arkansas and the Outlet, were attached to Oklahoma Territory for judicial purposes.

Indian Territory, roughly the eastern half of Oklahoma, consisted of the nations of the Five Civilized Tribes—Cherokee, Creek, Seminole, Choctaw, and Chickasaw. The only other Indians occupying Indian Territory were on the Quapaw reservation, a tiny region at the northeast corner of the Cherokee Nation, which had been given to the Quapaws, a few Senecas, a band of Shawnees, and small tribes of Miamis, Ottawas, Wyandottes, and Peorias. The Quapaw reservation contained not more than 1,500 Indians and cut no figure in the general statistics of the territory.

The Dawes Commission, which was in the midst of the allotment work among the Civilized Tribes, subdivided their estimated population as follows:

Full and mixed bloods	71,615
Freedmen	1,500
Intermarried whites	4,124
White non-citizens	443,217

"Mixed-blood" citizens were those of all degrees of Indian consanguinity—from half-bloods to the most remote 254th part, which meant almost total extinction. "Intermarried whites" were men and women who had married Indians, of whatever degree, and by such mar-

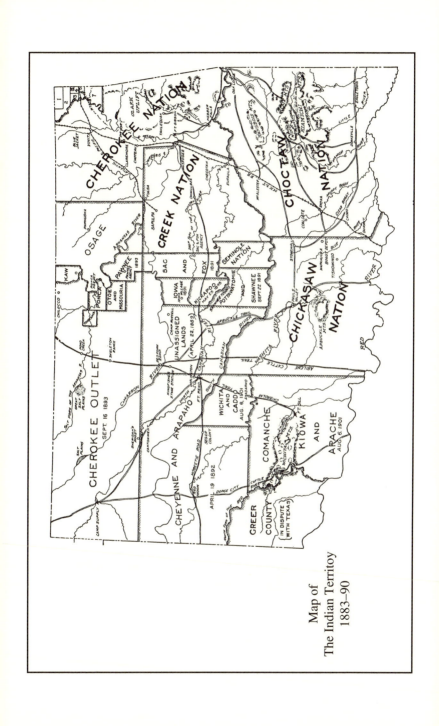

Map of
The Indian Territoy
1883–90

riage, had all the rights of citizenship and the community of property. "Freedmen" were African-Americans, once slaves of the Indians brought from the South during their removal to the territory, freed at the conclusion of the Civil War, and adopted into the various tribes with the full rights and privileges of national born Indian citizens.

Each civilized tribe, except the Seminoles (who operated under a brief organic law), had adopted a written constitution modeled after that of the United States—a governor or principal chief and assistant principal chief as executives, cabinet officers, and a legislative body or national council consisting of an upper house and a lower house which made laws for their people. Circuit and district judges and a supreme court adjudicated civil and criminal matters. District sheriffs preserved the peace and arrested criminals, aided by a national force of "light horsemen," which were peace officers similar to the Canadian Mounted Police and the Texas Rangers.

These governments were nominal, however. Despite the treaty covenants solemnly entered into guaranteeing the full right of self-government, the tribes were really under the control of the United States Department of the Interior, the federal district courts established in Indian Territory after 1889, and the federal court for the Western District of Arkansas at Fort Smith. Also, a United States Indian agent (Union Agency) at Muskogee, in the Creek Nation, was guardian over all the tribes.

Federal statutes prohibited any non-citizen from residing or trading in the Indian nations or reservations without paying a tax to the tribal treasuries and obtaining a license from the commissioner of Indian affairs or his agents. Such a license required a penal bond not to exceed $5,000, to be secured by one or more sureties, and renewed every three years. Any person attempting to reside or trade without a license was classified as an "intruder," to be fined $500 and his merchandise forfeited. Despite those statutes, the United States military and the Indian lighthorse had difficulty keeping out intruders.

Thousands of whites in every business and profession entered the territory as traders with the half-dozen railroad building projects launched by the government during the 1870s and 1880s. Many Indian settlements boomed as commercial centers. Ranchers and farmers also came to lease or sharecrop Indian lands, and their presence was protected by the government. The commissioner of Indian affairs even ruled that these residents could sell or bequeath the right of occupancy to business or resident lots to other white men. However, to draw boundaries or make surveys was punishable by heavy fines, and no purchase of land was valid.

Many avoided this law by intermarriage, thus

obtaining citizenship and the right to hold land and engage in business as though they were of Indian blood. To discourage intermarriage, and because such unions resulted in innumerable cases of divorce, separation, and desertion, the tribes set some license fees for marrying an Indian as high as $1,000. Other whites simply leased land from the Indians year after year until they virtually possessed it.

The great majority of whites were of the best quality, men with brains and capital; while they had no right or title to a foot of realty, they were a potent force in the commercial and industrial development of the territory. They appealed to the Indian agent at Muskogee, to the United States Department of the Interior, and to Congress, pointing out that they had been invited to come invest their capital and make homes yet were without any voice in the Indian governments, even to the extent of providing schools for their children. The appeal further claimed that, while the degree of intelligence among the Civilized Tribes was most gratifying, Indians were sadly in the minority, and it was certainly not in the best interests of society in general that the Indians' supremacy over more than 400,000 whites should be so complete as to wholly bar them in the management of local affairs and deny them title to their homes and safe proprietorship in business buildings—many large and costly—which they had erected.

Their appeals were supported by metropolitan centers in Kansas, Texas, Missouri, and Arkansas, to whose wholesalers full development of the territory's great resources meant millions of dollars where now there were only thousands. Secretary of the Interior Hoke Smith proposed abrogating the Indian treaties, abolishing tribal relations, and establishing a territorial government and extending the jurisdiction of the United States courts over the entire country. Governors of the adjoining states and the governor of Oklahoma Territory backed statehood for the "Twin Territories."

A board appointed by President Grover Cleveland in 1895 to appraise the lands and improvements of residents of the Cherokee Nation, reported 2,858 persons as non-claimant intruders. The Vinita *Indian Chieftain* of September 26 demanded, "Something will have to be done about this awful evil." The *Chieftain* was devoted to the interests of the Creeks, Seminoles, Chickasaws, and Choctaws, as well as the Cherokees. It was one of the most popular and influential newspapers in the territory, and many other Indian newspapers took up the banner.

However, the Muskogee *Phoenix* of October 3 observed that to remove all non-claimant intruders from the territory was "impracticable and would work distressing disaster to many worthy persons...and it should be remembered that the intruders can go into the courts and enjoin the execution of the orders of any of the departments, and delay effectively action indefinitely."

Governor John Brown of the Seminole Nation reported that his people were contented and prosperous. The only dissatisfaction and strife were over a mile-square pasture act which allowed heads of Indian families to erect fences for protection against invading cattlemen. The act had done little good, and the fences were to be taken down shortly. Though making no reference to intruding whites, he declared that justice and equity were nearer being dispensed in his nation than in the others.

Indian agent Dew M. Wisdom, at Muskogee, announced that he would remove intruders from the territory if the Indians would pay the freight. The Choctaw council appropriated $5,000 and the Cherokee council met in extra session to make a similar appropriation for that purpose. The Chickasaw court of claims ruled that a white man who had married into the tribe forfeited all his rights of citizenship if, after the decease of his Indian wife, he married a white woman. United States Indian agent Frank D. Baldwin, at Anadarko, ordered that every person who had not a perfect title to the rights and privileges of the Kiowa-Comanche-Apache reservation be removed from the reservation and along the Chickasaw border.

Thus the pot boiled. The scales would eventually tip in favor of the white invader, but not without continual and often violent pockets of resistance. The worst violence erupted in the Creek Nation during July and August of 1895.

THIRTEEN DAYS OF TERROR

Rob! Kill! Rape Their Women!

The Creek constitution was a short one. It provided for a principal chief and a second chief and a legislative body or national council of two houses—an upper house, or House of Kings, and a lower house, or House of Warriors—chosen by the voters of the nation. The nation was divided into six districts—Okmulgee, Coweta, Deep Fork, Muskogee, Wewoka and Eufaula—each with a judge chosen by the national council, a prosecuting attorney appointed by the principal chief, and a company of lighthorsemen elected by the voters of each district to maintain order. A supreme court of five members, chosen by the national council, was called the High Court. The rock-walled capitol building stood on the Deep Fork of the Canadian River near the center of the nation, and the village of Okmulgee had grown up around it. The "towns" in the nation, with their ancient clans and traditional procedures, were units of local government and political centers.

The people took their elections seriously. Feuds and factions, which had hindered the rebuilding of Indian Territory since the desolation of the Civil War, were less prevalent among the Creeks but were still the basis for political parties and issues. Speeches were made in the towns, in barns, log houses, under brush arbors and trees, to the tune of picnics and barbecues. Candidates were given every opportunity to explain why they should be chosen. The burning issue was the steady increase of intruders.

Intermarriages with whites were not permitted except by special act of the House of Kings and the House of Warriors. Consequently, there were few of them. That law, together with the nation's distance from state lines, should have lowered the danger of outside intrusion. But the adjoining Sac and Fox and Pawnee reservations were opened to settlement and attached to Oklahoma Territory in 1891 and 1893. Thus, with the extension of railroads, the Creek country's population of non-citizen railway employees, traders, farmers, and ranchmen increased to nearly 43,000, while the number of full- and mixed-blood citizens totaled about 9,000, freedmen, 5,500.

The Creeks contended that such use of their land was illegal. They would have stopped the practice by removing non-citizens and seizing their property, but the Fort Smith court had long

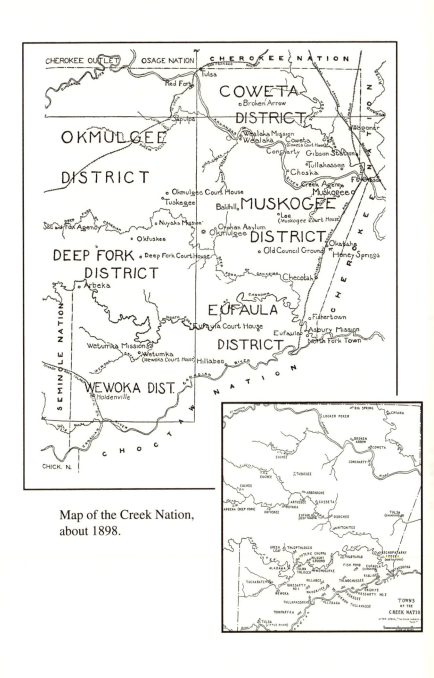

Map of the Creek Nation, about 1898.

since ruled against the Cherokees for attempting to use this method on cattlemen to enforce their grazing tax. The mere fact of a man's being in Indian country without a permit did not give Indian officers a right to seize or remove him or his property; the proper remedy was enforcement of the Intercourse Law by the federal government. That entailed district lighthorsemen furnishing the principal chief with the names of the intruders; the chief then reported them to the Indian agent at Muskogee, whose report went to the Department of the Interior, thence to the secretary of war, and finally to the army commander in the territory, who sent a detachment of soldiers to convey the intruders to the border of Kansas, Texas, or Arkansas. Creek authorities had little patience for the procedure and the inability to make the kind of reports required by the War Department.

The full-bloods watched with bewilderment while white men killed their game, fished their streams, and cut down their timber for exportation. During the early 1890s, the country was virtually stripped of the walnut that grew along the Arkansas River and branches of the Canadian. Much of it went to furniture factories in the East. One timber dealer, Louis Norburg, made walnut gunstocks, which he sold in great quantities to the government and abroad. With his profits, he established a large general store at Arbekochee (Arbeka) near the extreme northeastern corner of the Seminole Nation, and opened a freight line from Muskogee.

Most of the timber was cut at night and claimed by some bribed Creek citizen until spirited away. Some tribal district attorneys were not incorruptible, and the Indian agent at Muskogee declined to act unless the nation itself showed good faith by punishing its citizens who acted as go-betweens. Several timber thieves were arrested and their logs seized.

Early in 1895, the prosecuting attorneys were ordered to sell all down timber in their districts at public auction for the benefit of the tribe. The attorney for the Wewoka district contracted to sell all of its down timber to a dealer without offering it to the public. By some clever transactions, the timber passed into the hands of Norburg. When Norburg's next shipment of gunstocks reached Eufaula, the Eufaula district attorney attached it, but the shipment went out. The Wewoka district judge complained to Agent Wisdom. Wisdom examined the bills of sale, blamed the Wewoka district attorney, assured Norburg that interference with his property by Indian authorities was unwarranted and prohibited, and told the judge that Norburg, as a United States citizen, was out of his jurisdiction. The Wewoka district attorney was removed from office, but the affair added to the boil of tribal politics.

Of greater disgust to all classes of Creeks was

the occupation of their land by intruding cattlemen. The Coweta district between the Arkansas River and Cherokee Nation was almost entirely occupied. The mile-square pasture act seemed to be the solution. However, as in the Seminole Nation, the act proved useless and inoperable. Along the borders, the Indians themselves formed pasture companies to lease their fenced areas in blocks for grazing, and so many rival claimants to desirable tracts filed suits in the tribal courts that the law was repealed.

A flood of declarations against cattlemen for not paying the tribal tax caused the prosecuting attorney of the Muskogee district to institute proceedings against H.B. Spaulding; M.L. Minter and T.F. Meagher (both intermarried white men); F.B. Severs, of Muskogee; George Shannon and Company of Texas; and Benton Callahan, a prominent rancher on Grave Creek, southeast of Okmulgee. All six were convicted and fined a total of $50,000. Severs and Meagher got off by voluntarily paying the required taxes. Minter and Spauldlng appealed to the federal court on the ground that they were United States citizens. Shannon and Company refused to pay a $30,000 fine; the lighthorse seized l0,000 cattle to satisfy the judgment, and United States citizens from whom the company took the cattle produced a mortgage and sought an injunction against the Creek officers. Other United States citizens intervened with a mortgage given by Benton

Callahan, and prevented execution of the judgment against some 2,000 cattle on his U-Bar ranch.

While the tribal and federal governments clashed over their conflicting interests and policies, 100,000 longhorns continued to graze on the nation's prairies, and the white population increased. Though the tax and lease laws were enforced better than before, the Dawes Severalty Act and approaching dissolution of the government of all Five Civilized Tribes paralyzed the Creeks. Creek methods of self-government were generally disregarded, and glowing pictures were painted of statehood and the advantages of casting their burdens upon the shoulders of the United States.

By the end of the grazing season of 1895, Creeks from nearly every town in the nation had petitioned their chiefs to find a way to throw out the white man. One group led by John Buck, a full-blood member of the Euchee band and a prominent politician, took their appeal directly to the old rock-walled capitol at Okmulgee, where the two branches of the remnant Creek sovereignty still held sway. The national council promised a solution, but it must be peaceful and would take time.

John Buck's son, Rufus, claimed he knew a quicker way to make the whites take notice: Rob! Kill! Rape their women!

Corporate Outlaws

Rufus Buck was twenty-two years old, a stocky full-blood with wild black hair and piercing black eyes. He was born and raised on the Buck family farm in the area where Duck and Snake creeks joined as a tributary to the Arkansas River southeast of Tulsey Town (Tulsa), near present Leonard.

Atop a hill south of the river and commanding a fine view of its fertile valley, stood the commodious domed brick building of the Wealaka Mission, a boarding school for Indian children.[1] Under Creek law, the community furnished the building, and the tribe appointed and paid the superintendent and teacher. The site had been established in 1881, and was also the location of a trading post and post office owned by Chief Samuel W. Brown, a mixed-blood Euchee. Daniel "Goob" Childers, a captain of the lighthorse in the Okmulgee district, operated a ferry down the hill from the mission on the Arkansas.[2]

Rufus Buck attended Wealaka Mission for a time while in his teens. The superintendent was S.P. Callahan, father of Benton Callahan of the U-Bar ranch southeast of Okmulgee. Children attending the school were not allowed to speak Creek or any Indian language, even on the playground, which was "very painful" to them. Parents who brought their children to the mission—sometimes 100 miles by horseback—often returned home to find their children had preceded them. Rufus was a "mean" boy, to the point that Superintendent Callahan expelled him.[3]

Thereafter, Rufus became a hanger-on, consorting with two young law-breakers not quite his age—Lewis Davis, a Euchee full-blood, and Luckey Davis (no relation to Lewis), a "coal black negro," Creek freedman, and considered one of the most "fiendish and dangerous" desperados to infest Indian Territory.[4]

J.I. Belford, a Tulsa old-timer interviewed in 1976, remembered Lewis and Luckey Davis well. J.I.'s father, N.R. "Newt" Belford, a Missourian, had brought his wife and three small children to the Creek Nation in a covered wagon in 1893. J.I. was then eight, his sister five, and his brother two years old. The family boarded with relatives in Tulsa until Newt could find a suitable site for a trading post.

A cousin introduced Newt to A.D. and Adaline

Orcutt, prominent ranchers in the area, who helped him obtain a site about six miles north of present Beggs. Newt built a house first, then a store, which he stocked with merchandise purchased from a Tulsa wholesaler and opened for business in 1894. He soon added a post office, designated "Orcutt, I.T." in honor of A.D. and Adaline Orcutt. J.I. had the chore of back-stamping incoming letters, and thus he and his father met Lewis and Luckey Davis.

The pair came to the store with twenty-three hogs they wanted to sell. Newt suspected that the animals were stolen, but Lewis Davis insisted that he and Luckey had "raised them back in the woods." Newt hadn't been to the bank in Tulsa lately and had only twenty-one dollars cash on hand. He offered to pay that amount for the hogs and make up the balance in trade at the store. Lewis Davis decided to take the difference in Hostetter's Bitters (a popular alcoholic drink of the time), and accepted the twenty-one silver dollars.

J.I., an interested spectator, saw Lewis furtively stuff the big coins into a secret pocket on his cartridge belt. Then the pair gathered up their bottles of bitters and left.

A short time later, Jensie George and her husband who lived nearby, came to the store, identified their hogs, and herded them back home.

The next day a passerby brought a cartridge belt and two hats to the store. He had found them in the woods not far away and thought the owners would be looking for their property. J.I. told Newt to look inside the secret coin pocket on the belt, and the elder Belford "was surprised when he found $21." Lewis and Luckey Davis had gone on a "bitters binge" and left the gun belt and hats under a tree."[5] They never returned to claim their property, but it would not be the Belfords' last encounter with Lewis and Luckey Davis.

One night several weeks later, the two hog thieves, accompanied by Rufus Buck, appeared at Chief Brown's store at Wealaka. The chief's son, W.S. Brown, was alone in the store and recalled, "They rode up and bought some tobacco and a rope; the next night a prized yellow cutting horse was stolen from a farmer in the area and led away."[6] The horse with the rope was recovered, but the three were never charged with this crime.

However, deputy United States marshals arrested Rufus Buck for introducing whiskey into Indian Territory, and he served a ninety-day sentence in the United States jail at Fort Smith. During his confinement, he was an "exemplary prisoner and was made a trusty."[7]

In jail Rufus met Crawford "Cherokee Bill" Goldsby. He had followed closely the antics of the marauding Bill Cook-Cherokee Bill gang during 1894 and early 1895. Cook had been sent to the Albany, New York, prison. Goldsby was waiting to be hanged for murdering an innocent bystander during a robbery at Lenapah, Cherokee Nation. Shortly after Buck's release, Goldsby went on a rampage in the jail, attempting a wholesale delivery of prisoners, and killed Guard Lawrence Keating. Rufus Buck looked on Goldsby as a hero, thrilled at the public attention Goldsby received, and as theorized by some, wanted to bask in the desperado's blood-stained glory.

A congressional act of March 1, 1895, had divided Indian Territory into Northern, Central and Southern dlstricts, with United States courts headquartered at Muskogee, McAlester, and Ardmore, respectively. Samuel Morton Rutherford, "a slender man with a red mustache and eyes that fascinate," was United States marshal of the northern district at Muskogee. He was a lawyer and United States commissioner at Atoka, Choctaw Nation, when the attorney general in Washington endorsed him as "the right man for the suppression of train robbers." Within months after his appointment, he had delivered more than a score of notorious bandits to the Fort Smith court to be dealt with by the "hanging judge," Isaac Charles Parker.[8]

Rutherford and his deputies chose to deliver all major law violators to Fort Smith, even where jurisdiction rested with the Muskogee court. "While this is not obligatory upon them," observed the Muskogee *Phoenix*, "it helps to

Samuel Morton Rutherford, United States Marshal,
Northern District of Indian Territory at Muskogee

keep down the worst lawlessness and decreases the small crimes. [The officers] are entitled to the thanks of the people for this course."[9]

John Buck had done nothing to curb his son's wantonness. Within days after Rufus was released from the Fort Smith Jail, Deputy Marshal Mark Moore arrested him "for being mixed up in some cattle stealing" near Okmulgee. While Moore "went after the other thieves," he left Rufus in the custody of poseman Zeke Wilson, at Okmulgee. Wilson, in conveying his prisoner through the streets of the town—"the desperate character of his charge being not known"—was not on the alert. Rufus Buck was. At an opportune moment, he snatched Wilson's pistol from his belt, "and leveling it on him, defiantly walked away."[10]

When next heard from, Buck was riding with "four sullen, fiendish young fellows": Lewis and Luckey Davis, and two Creek full-bloods of the Cussetah tribal town, Tulsey—Sam Sampson and Maomi July. "None is over 18 years old, yet their crimes partake of the savagery practiced by the wild Indians upon the early settlers of America."[11]

Sampson and July, like Lewis and Luckey Davis, were petty criminals. They were also perverts who liked to molest women. None of the four cared for Rufus Buck's grudge against whites, or even the money and valuables he promised. They had thieved so often they made a joke of it, and would play cruel tricks on their victims.

The gang brought a depraved change in Rufus Buck. All his hate for whites surfaced as he led his cohorts from the brush thickets of Snake Creek, Sunday evening, July 28, 1895, on a spree of destruction.

Murder of Deputy Marshall John Garrett

The Buck gang was heavily armed with six-shooters and Winchesters. Rufus Buck's arsenal included the semi-automatic pistol he had taken from Zeke Wilson in his escape at Okmulgee. But the gang needed better horses and good saddles.

About two o'clock Monday morning, July 29, the busy little town of Checotah, thirty some miles southeast of Okmulgee on the Missouri, Kansas and Texas (Katy) Railroad, awoke to a storm of gunshots and the cry of "Fire!" The middle of the business district was in flames, and everybody rushed to aid in checking the fire or to save their property.

The fire, which originated in H.G. Turner's livery stable, spread rapidly to the adjoining Byers & Leven drygoods and toward a long frame building used by Spaulding & Company to store implements, grain, and other feed stuffs. Mitchell

Perry's barber shop stood about midway between the fire and Spaulding's warehouse. Had the flames "lapped to Spaulding's," probably not a building in the two business blocks would have been left standing.

"Every energy was exerted" to save Perry's establishment. "But the fire fighters were hampered by the want of water. Water was drawn from neighboring cisterns and wells, and the bucket brigade kept wet blankets over Spaulding's and a stream of water on the barber shop."

Mr. Borden, agent for a fire extinguisher company, happened to be in town with some of his equipment. He had "a good opportunity to test its value, and did so." Each time the fire caught the Spaulding structure, Borden "smothered it out. He had a limited amount of acid to "charge with, but he fought the fire bravely." The intense heat burned his face, hands and back, and he inhaled so much smoke he was in bed under the care of a physician the next day.

Spaulding & Company lost several hundred dollars' worth of implements and grain. Byers & Leven saved most of their merchandise by removing it from the store. Turner saved his horses and vehicles, but his harness and other items incidental to the livery business were destroyed. "Some excellent saddles were in the stable before the fire, but neither the stirrups nor saddle irons could be found." The fire was of incendiary origin; apparently thieves had taken the saddles and then set the blaze "to hide their crime."

That theory strengthened at daylight when Dr. West reported that, during the night, someone had stolen several horses from his pasture a mile west of town. Apparently the thieves had taken the horses, then finished equipping themselves from Turner's stable before setting it aflame.[1]

There was no clue to the thievery or incendiary, but developments during the days that followed convinced Checotah's citizens that it had been the work of the Buck gang.

About dusk, Tuesday, July 30, Rufus Buck, Lewis Davis, and Luckey Davis visited "Big Nellie's place" in Okmulgee.[2] The town had two stores, one a two-story establishment which stocked clothing on the upper floor and was part of cattleman F.B. Severs' mercantile chain out of Muskogee; the other, a one-story building at Seventh and Morton streets, operated by an Indian trader named Parkinson.[3] Around eight o'clock, Buck remarked to his pals that it was about time for Parkinson to close, and the three departed Big Nellie's, "secreting themselves in a barn back of the store, where their horses were hidden."[4]

Parkinson did considerable grocery business with the Indians, a government payment had just been made to them, and many had settled their accounts during the day. "Parkinson had a great deal of cash on hand, and the supposition was that the outlaws intended to rob his store."5

A fly in the ointment was John Garrett, a freedman, who was Okmulgee's town marshal, a deputy United States marshal, and a member of the Creek lighthorse. Garrett knew that Buck was still wanted by Deputy Marshal Moore, and on a tip that the fugitive had visited Big Nellie's, Garrett went hunting for him.

Rufus' mother and father happened to be in town that day. They had been seen at Parkinson's, and Garrett went there to question them about their son's whereabouts. Elijah Grayson, a customer, told the marshal that John Buck had gone on some errand, but Rufus' mother was "sitting on the back steps of the store." With Grayson at his heels, Garrett "passed out the back door to question Mrs. Buck, not knowing that the outlaws were about." He was only a few steps into the yard when Rufus Buck leaped from the barn door, a pistol in hand, and "opened on him a volley of lead." Garrett "fell at Buck's mother's feet...shot through the left breast and one leg."6

Grayson stood frozen. He later testified, "Buck threatened to shoot me too if I made any outcry."7 The outlaw then yelled, "Bring my horse." Lewis and Luckey Davis rode from the barn.

Buck mounted, and they left town "whooping in outlaw fashion."8 Policeman Alec Berryhill was standing in the drugstore down the street, talking to Doctor Bell, the proprietor. They heard the gunfire and whoops and glimpsed three riders sweep past the window. As they stepped from the drugstore, "a man ran up and told Doctor Bell to hurry to Parkinson's, as the marshal had been shot and needed attention....When Dr. Bell got to the wounded man, he told Doctor Bell he had been shot by Rufus Buck, then went into a coma until he died at 3 o'clock the next morning."[9]

A man named Robert Thomas "picked up the shells where the shooting was done."[10] It was determined later that Buck had used Zeke Wilson's pistol to kill Garrett.[11]

Berryhill led a posse through the countryside all night in a fruitless search for the killers. Posses were still scouring the Okmulgee area Saturday night, August 3, when the "Buck gang squared a grudge they had against the Pigeon family of Indians by burning Dave Pigeon's home and the houses on the place of Jesse Pigeon."[12] The Pigeons allegedly were white sympathizers.

Criminality Without Parallel

The gang dashed northward. Sunday morning, August 4, while roaming near Natura, nine miles east of Orcutt, they spotted an old gentleman named Ayers and his comely young daughter, who were moving across the country in a wagon. They were white people and had been living in the Seminole Nation.

"Buck and one of his clan [Luckey Davis] met them, at the point of guns, and ordered the girl to get off the wagon. She and her father pleaded with the outlaws, but they threatened to kill both unless their demands were complied with. The girl was carried a few steps from the roadside where one of the outlaws raped her. She was then permitted to return to the wagon. Just then three others [Lewis Davis, Sampson and July] came up, and they in turn each satisfied their lust on the poor girl in the presence of her father." Ayers and his daughter were then told to go on.

"The story, as we learn it," concluded the Muskogee *Phoenix*, "is most revolting....The girl, we understand, received critical injuries."[1]

Riding east to Berryhill Creek, within eight miles of Okmulgee, the gang met Jim Shafey, "a walnut log man." Rufus Buck knocked him from the saddle with the stock of his Winchester. After "threatening and abusing" him for nearly an hour, the gang "discussed the advisability of killing him." July suggested they take a vote. The vote was three to two in Shafey's favor. So they "robbed him of his horse, saddle and bridle, $50 in money and a gold watch," and the terrified timber dealer fled on foot.[2]

The gang rode fast from Berryhill Creek. Cattlemen ate at Rufus Buck like white settlers and timber dealers, and he was remembering the time rancher Benton Callahan's father had expelled him from Wealaka Mission. At dusk Sunday, the gang reached Callahan's U-Bar ranch southeast of Okmulgee.

Callahan and a black cowboy, Sam Houston, had rounded up some cattle for shipping and were driving them along the creek when the ravagers swooped down on them. They did not "recognize the riders at first, they were coming at such great speed. Bang! Bang! went their guns." Houston's horse died under him. The cowboy tried to escape on foot, and they brought him down with a bullet through the shoulder. Callahan "felt a hot piercing sensation" in his left ear, and when he saw blood running down his shirt, he knew they had "shot off a part of it."[3]

The outlaws swept around him, and assuming that Houston was dead, Buck snarled: "Your ol' man kicked me out of school—I ought to have the boys kill you too!"

July suggested a vote, but none was taken. Buck took a few dollars the rancher had in his pockets, his horse, saddle, hat, and boots. Then the gang rode off at a breakneck speed towards the west.

"There I was," said Callahan, "my man lying in a pool of blood, his horse dead, the cattle stampeded in several directions. I was barefooted and had some distance to go before I could get help to get my man to a doctor. Finally, I managed to get a wagon, put some hay in it…loaded my man in the wagon and started the trip to Checotah, the nearest town."[4]

As news of the attack spread through the countryside, several men set out for the scene. They met Callahan on the way and "carried the wounded cowboy on to Checotah…where his death is daily expected."[5] A later report stated, "Sam Houston is improving under the care of Drs. Stewart and Davis, and will recover."[6]

William Frank Jones, a twenty-three-year-old deputy working under his uncle, Deputy United States Marshal Jesse H. Jones, in Checotah, took two possemen to the U-Bar ranch, camped that night, and next morning trailed the gang north-west to within ten miles of Sapulpa.

While Jones and his posse slept, the Bucks were busy. Shortly before midnight, they "visited the ranch of Gus Chambers, on Duck Creek, to steal fresh horses." Chambers resisted with a shotgun, and they "filled his house with lead."[7]

Mrs. Dollie Garretson, who worked for the Chambers family at the time, recalled: "About 100 shots were exchanged. The woman and small boy [Chambers' wife and son] hid under the bed. When daylight came the Bucks left without the horses. People found eight bullets in the bed under which the woman and boy hid—but weren't hit."[8]

Monday morning, August 5, Deputy Jones and posse picked up the trail and followed it across Duck Creek to a country road leading to Wealaka. A young man and a fourteen-year-old boy in a wagon came whipping down the road toward them, shouting that the boy's mother was in the hands of the Bucks!

The white mother—Mrs. Mary Wilson, an elderly widow—had been living on a place about four miles southeast of the Buck farm, and was moving her household goods in two wagons to a new place she had rented a few miles distant. She was driving the lead wagon, followed by her son, Charles, and Freddie Malcolm, a neighbor hired to drive the second wagon, when the Bucks burst from the wooded roadside on sweating mounts, their jeans dust-caked, vests and hat brims flapping, long-shanked spurs jangling, and six-shooters drawn.

First, they rifled the woman's possessions. After taking her money and a few baubles that appealed to them, "the boys were made to drive on with one wagon, while they kept the other wagon and the woman." Then Luckey Davis, the little Creek-African, put his revolver to the woman's head and ordered her to "strip down." "Stand by, fellahs," he challenged his companions, "an' watch how a expert makes love."

He ravished the woman while she sobbed helplessly, and the others nodded approval. Afterwards, all five fired at her heels as she fled into the underbrush to "'hide her nakedness and shame." There the officers found her, "half-dead from fright and abuse."[9]

Charles carried his mother to the wagon and took her home. Young Malcolm went in the other wagon for a doctor. The woman recovered, but remained practically an invalid the rest of her days.

While his possemen searched the timber for a new trail, Jones proceeded to the Buck farm, but found no one at home. He "lay in wait around the house, no contact." Finally, Buck's sister came along, carrying a pistol. She pulled the gun on Jones, but he disarmed her. She denied having seen her brother, or knowing where the gang was hiding.[10]

The Bucks blithely rode south again. "A white

John B. "Buck" McDonough, Assistant United States District Attorney at Fort Smith, prosecuted the Buck Gang for rape and murder.

man employed to break sod land for Monty Tiger adjoining the Half Moon ranch between Okmulgee and Checotah...was camping at his work Monday evening when the outlaws rode up, helped themselves to what they wanted and killed him."[11]

Monday night, another rape was charged to the fiends. "They went to a place west of Checotah where a schoolma'm was boarding...took possession of the house and outraged the white teacher. Whose home it was or who was the victim is not learned."[12]

Enumerating the gang's criminality from July 29 to August 5, the Muskogee *Phoenix* said, "It is without parallel in the history of Indian Territory....The people in the Okmulgee country are intimidated and in constant fear of being...abused by them. It is not considered safe for women to go about, and many of the homes are under guard of men folk....The town of Okmulgee has its guns greased [in event of a revisit] to that place."[13]

Tuesday morning, August 6, Assistant United States District Attorney John B. "Buck" McDonough, at Fort Smith, charged before United States Commissioner Stephen Wheeler that "Rufus Buck, Lewis Davis and Luckey Davis, did, in the Indian Territory, within the Creek Nation, Western District of Arkansas, on or about the 30th day of July 1895, feloniously, wilfully, premeditatively and of their malice aforethought kill and murder John Garrett, a deputy marshal, against the peace and dignity of the United States...and I pray a writ." Among the witnesses endorsed were Newton Armstrong, Elijah Grayson and Robert Thomas.[14]

Commissioner Wheeler issued a capias (warrant) which was delivered to United States Marshal George J. Crump, of Fort Smith. Crump dispatched copies to Marshal Rutherford at Muskogee. Rutherford put Deputy Marshals Samuel Haynes and N.B. Irwin into the field, with instructions that "information as to what witnesses will state should be procured from personal interviews, and not from hearsay."[15]

On a complaint filed by Deputy Marshal Jesse H. Jones of Checotah, Commissioner Wheeler issued a second capias charging that Rufus Buck, Lewis Davis, Luckey Davis, Sam Sampson and Maomi July "did on the 4th day of August 1895...in the Creek Nation...make an assault upon Sam Houston, a Negro and not an Indian...with intent then and there feloniously, wilfully and of their malice aforethought to kill...."[16]

Marshal Rutherford, the Muskogee *Phoenix* reported, had announced from his office that, "out of a total of eighteen deputies in the [Northern] district, he now has twelve of them in the field...to put 'Buck & Co.' out of business...and claims they are going to camp on their trail until they find them....News has just come to town that the [Ayers] girl the gang raped has died."[17]

The afternoon of August 6, even as Rutherford was marshaling his forces, the gang appeared near Snake Creek, northeast of Orcutt, at the home of Henry Hassan.

Outrage at Snake Creek

Henry Hassan was an honest, hard-working man who had virtually carved a little farm from the timbered and brush-covered bottoms of Snake Creek, fenced it with rails he had split himself, erected a small barn for his livestock, and built a comfortable log house flanked by a brush arbor for protection from the winter snows and summer heat. His family consisted of a wife, Rosetta, a well-proportioned, kindly woman of thirty, and three small children. Living with them was Rosetta's aged mother.

The Hassan's closest neighbor was a young farmer named Dick Ryan (also spelled "Rhine" in court records). Ryan lived a short distance up the creek, occasionally worked for the family as a hired hand, and accommodated them by dropping off their mail or any staples they might need when he returned from visits to the Belford trading post and post office at Orcutt.

It was harvest season. Hassan relaxed on a cot

beneath the brush arbor. Nearby, his wife was preparing fruit for the family larder. The old mother pampered the children. When Hassan saw the five riders turn from the trail through the front gate, he supposed, living in a secluded area where travelers seldom passed, that they were hunters.

As they drew nearer, he whispered to his wife, "Rufus Buck! Get in the house, Rosetta—all of you." Rosetta hurried inside with her mother and the children.

Hassan and Buck had had a minor disagreement about the latter's grudge against whites and the lax enforcement of Creek tribal laws. Hassan had thought nothing more of it. He hadn't seen Buck since Buck had "gone on the rampage," and hoped the outlaw also had forgotten the matter.

Hassan greeted Buck pleasantly. Buck asked for water, and when Hassan arose and started to the well for a fresh pail, Luckey Davis signaled for the others to close around their victim. A few weeks previously, Hassan had asked Luckey to please close the gates when he passed through the farm. Luckey had told him, "I got more important things to do; I oughta tear down the whole damn fence." Hassan could only guess what ill will Davis bore him now.

The farmer began backing slowly toward the corner of the house, hoping to reach its cover, then enter the back door, inside of which stood his Winchester. He gained the corner safely and ran to the door. As he started to enter, he was met by Maomi July. July had leaped from his mount, dashed through the house, secured the coveted rifle, and now brushed Hassan's face with its muzzle. Sam Sampson, who had pursued the farmer around the house, covered him with a six-shooter.

With vile oaths, the pair hustled their captive back to the arbor. Rufus Buck shoved him onto the cot. "Try anything else," he warned, "and we'll blow your brains out both ears!" Then he called Rosetta Hassan to the door and ordered, "Cook us a good meal, woman, and be damn quick about it!" While the old mother shushed the children, Rosetta put more wood in the cook stove and hastened to prepare meat and eggs and black coffee.

Leaving Luckey Davis to guard Hassan outside, the rest of the gang rifled the house, top to bottom. They appropriated $5.95 in cash, a suit of Hassan's clothes, and various articles of feminine apparel, snickering and cavorting about with the undergarments of the poor women. Then they hunkered at the table and gulped down food and coffee, staring at Rosetta Hassan in ominous silence. The meal finished, they ushered the old mother and the children outside under the arbor and stood guard over them and Hassan while Luckey Davis went in to dinner.

The smelly, sullen outlaw wolfed down his

food, eyeing Rosetta's figure, then told her, "You have to go with me." The woman begged him not to take her away from her babies, and he replied, "We'll throw the God damn brats in the creek!"

He marched her outside and commanded her to mount his horse, only desisting when she declared she could not ride. "Then we go to the barn," he said, and remarked to Henry Hassan, "I'm gonna give you somethin' besides gates to think about." He thrust the muzzle of his Winchester close to the woman's head.

Rosetta hesitated. Tears welled in her eyes, but believing she and the rest of the family would be killed if she refused, she finally complied. Inside the barn, the brute ordered her to take off her clothes and lie down. What occurred afterwards was repeated one, two, three, four times—the slobbering, swearing Rufus Buck, Lewis Davis, Sampson, and July each taking his turn—while at all times three of them remained ready to send bullets crashing through the husband's brain should he attempt to remonstrate.

The five then turned to the next phase of their darkest, foulest exploit. Lewis Davis knew that Hassan was a professional buck-and-wing dancer, but suffered occasionally from chills that made his muscles cramp. A soaking in the cold waters of the spring on Snake Creek, two miles away, would stop his dancing for some time. Buck ordered Hassan to take off his boots and socks.

Dick Ryan, knowing nothing of the tragedy being enacted, drove up at that moment in his wagon. The entire gang roared with laughter at the expression on the hired man's face, and voted unanimously to include him in the program.

Mounting their horses, they marched both men ahead of them to Snake Creek. There they amused themselves by making Hassan dance, firing random shots at his bare feet to keep the jig lively. Next, they threw him in the spring, then dragged him out, and compelled the two men to wrestle and fight each other until both dropped from exhaustion.

Buck gave Hassan a parting warning: "If you ever appear in court against us, our friends will kill you."

To his pals, he remarked, "After this day white men will think ten times before comin' on Indian land." The others whooped in agreement, and the gang galloped away.

Hassan and Ryan hurried painfully back to the house. The old mother, virtually helpless from the infirmities of age, still sat beneath the arbor where the gang had left her, trying to quiet the crying children. Rosetta was missing. "Where is she?" cried Hassan. "Where did she go?"

The mother pointed toward the cornfield nearby. Hassan then saw the tracks where his wife had dragged herself into the field to hide. He found her between two corn rows, trying to cover her body with a ragged remnant of her bloody skirt and babbling half out of mind. Gently, he carried her to the house. Ryan went for a doctor.

It was two days before the woman became rational enough to hug her husband and babies, and cry, "Thank God, we are still alive!"[1]

Battle at Flat Rock

News of the attack on the Hassans spread like wildfire. "People in the central portion of the nation became panic stricken…women and children were congregated and put under guard, and the men—Indians, whites and Negroes—went out by the hundreds to hunt the gang down." Deputy Marshals Samuel Haynes and N.B. Irwin organized posses to "hound the gang to death," and Captain Edmund Harry entered the field with his Creek lighthorse in full force. Deputy Marshal Jesse H. Jones arrived from Checotah with another posse the next morning. "Every hill, every bottom and every trail for miles around is being critically searched, and there is hardly a hope for the escape of the brutes."[1]

The Buck gang kept on the move. At Orcutt, they found young J.I. Belford and his six-year-old brother minding the store. Newt Belford had joined one of the posses and had the foresight to take the contents of the cash drawer with him, believing that his young sons would not be harmed. The outlaws gorged themselves with big slices off a wheel of cheese, cans of sardines, and crackers. Then they plucked a pair of boots off a center post of the store, cut about a yard of quarter-inch rope from a coil to tie the boots together for saddle riders, stuffed the legs with rifle and six-shooter cartridges, and rode into the Tuskegee hills.[2]

About three o'clock Wednesday afternoon, August 7, the gang crossed the North Fork of the Canadian and held up the big Norburg & Company store in the little sawmill village of Arbekochee, taking twenty dollars cash and several hundred dollars' worth of jewelry, boots, clothing, guns, ammunition, canned goods and candies. Doubling back across the North Fork, they robbed a grocery store in the hamlet of McDermott. Finding no cash, they broke the glass from display cases, turned over fixtures, and dumped flour and sugar all over the floor. Shortly afterwards, they struck a general store just west of well-guarded Okmulgee, operated by a man named Knobble. They bound Knobble hand and foot, stuffed two gunny sacks with coffee, meat, tobacco, and more clothing, and continued northward into the hills.[3]

It was great fun, but it wouldn't last.

At noon, August 8, the gang stopped in a little

> **... BUCK AN OUTLAW CHIEF**
>
> **... Week He Has Made an Unparalleled Record of Brutal Crime.**
>
> Rufus Buck is a young Uchee Indian, who, until a few weeks ago, was almost unheard of out of his local beat. Only last week he become a defiant outlaw chief, and since then the record of crime by his gang has been startling for its brutality and rapid changes. Marshal Rutherford's deputies have been busy rounding up horse thieves in the Okmulgee country for some while, and four men charged with this offense have been recently put in jail here. About three weeks ago Deputy Mark Moore, of Okmulgee, and Deputy Wilson, of Muskogee, arrested Rufus Buck for being mixed up in some cattle stealing out there. The marshals carried him to Okmulgee and left him in keeping of a guard while they went after

The August 8, 1895, Muskogee *Phoenix* reported the Buck gang's depredations.

glade near Flatrock Creek, a mile and a half southwest of present Preston (seven miles north of Okmulgee). They drop-reined their mounts to switch flies and graze on the half-dead prairie grass, then hunkered in a group to inventory the proceeds of their crimes. Immediately they began arguing over how the plunder should be divided.

At length Rufus Buck told the others he would divide the loot himself, and since he was the leader, he would take first choice. The others didn't like that and started quarreling again.

From where the gang sat, the ground sloped upward about 200 feet to a knob called "Flat Rock." The knob covered about one-fourth of an acre, from which the country could be viewed for miles around. A sentry posted there could have easily warned of the approach of any posse before it got within shooting distance. But the outlaws felt too secure for caution, and were totally engaged in their plunder.

"Goods and ammunition were scattered over the ground," when they were discovered and fired upon by a squad of seven manhunters— Deputy Marshals Haynes and Irwin, and Captain Harry, Tom Grayson, George Brown, Sandy Tobler, and an old Indian named "Shansey," of the lighthorse police. The onslaught was "so sudden, so unexpected" that it drove the outlaws from their horses. "'With a muffled oath, each grabbed his rifle, and with the a agility of panthers," rushed for the top of Flat Rock. One outlaw bullet "passed through Captain Harry's hat, and grazed his head. The force of the shot knocked him from his horse and stunned him, but it brought no blood." The officers dismounted, and "a fight on foot lasted for fifteen or twenty minutes," before the outlaws gained the vantage of the top of the hill. A posse of citizens composed of Stanford, Thomas, and William Berryhill, J.A. McMullen, W.H. Hines, Harry Walker, John Gossett, and J.H. Minter, led by C.G. Sloan, had "gone out to reconnoiter in search of a trail" following the Knobble store robbery. Attracted by the shooting, they came up to Flat Rock from the opposite direction. Thus, "an impassable cordon was formed around the bandits."[4]

The battle raged into the afternoon. The Bucks pumped volleys at the pursuers spread out below until their magazines were empty; then they would retire to the center of the knob, reload, creep back to the edge and fire again. The officers and possemen kept up a rattling reply and ascended the slope by degrees, hugging rocks, bushes, and even the grass roots, as safety permitted. The constant gunfire echoed through the countryside, and nearly 100 others who were hunting the outlaws arrived on the scene and joined the fight.

At Fort Smith, an unusually large number of petty cases filled Judge Parker's docket. Several had been disposed of during the morning, and just as the court reconvened at one o'clock, a dispatch came stating that a "big posse" had engaged the Buck gang in a "roundup" and they had "no chance for escape."[5]

Harman, in *Hell on the Border*, describes how the news was received in Fort Smith:

> Everybody had heard of the Buck gang....Their acts had filled the people of the city and entire country with horror...."The Buck Gang" was upon everybody's lips. The news reached the court house. There were in the yard and corridors over 400 persons who had been summoned as witnesses [or to] listen idly to the numerous petty cases....Inside the court room word was passed from lip to lip...and almost instantly all was a-bustle. A bailiff whispered the news to Judge Parker; and he nodded pleasantly, called for order in the court and proceeded with the regular business. Soon another dispatch; it read:
>
> "Deputy marshals and Indians are engaged in a hand to hand conflict with the Buck gang."
>
> Like a flash the contents of this second dispatch found its way to every nook and cranny of the city. In the court room the bustle increased; attorneys for once forgot to ask questions, and witnesses to answer them, and again and again Judge Parker called for the bailiffs to preserve order. His tone was kindly, however, and he seemed to join in with the crowd in secret exultation at the fact that the murderous and unholy gang had been tracked to their lair. All through the afternoon this eager uneasiness continued and Judge Parker's voice would sing out ever and anon.
>
> "The United States against —————; Mr. McDonough are you ready in this case?"

"Yes, your honor."

"Bring in the prisoner; swear the witnesses; order in the court!" And when the court finally adjourned everyone hurried to the streets to learn of the fight and gathered in little knots to discuss the probable outcome [Harman, pp. 499–500].

Shortly after dark, a third dispatch brought word that the battle was over and four of the five Bucks had been taken alive.

The deputy marshals and Captain Harry's lighthorse had reached the rim of Flat Rock. "The outlaws retreated, running from tree to tree...shooting about 25 times each as they ran." In the dusk, the "pumping of lead, with the accompanying flashes, gave the appearance of a constant blaze of fire, and the smoke at times hung over the knob until the belligerents were hidden from each other." Finally, the Indian "Shansey" rose bravely to his feet, and shouted, "I've had enough of this!" He pushed a dynamite cartridge into his old rifle that was built to stand only the force of exploding gunpowder—something probably no other man present would have dared to do—took aim at the tree behind which Buck was standing, and fired. The explosive shattered bark from the tree, and a fragment of metal cut Buck's cartridge belt. As it fell to the ground, the outlaw leader threw away his Winchester and fled with the rest of his equally demoralized gang down the opposite side of the knob into the arms of Sloan's posse. [6]

A BIG FIGHT, BUT BLOODLESS.

The Rufus Buck Gang of Rapists and Outlaws in Jail.

Rufus Buck and his gang of outlaws, except one, are in limbo at Fort Smith, and they are glad to be within its protecting walls. Hundreds of men, whites, Indians and negroes, in the central portion of the nation, turned out to hunt them. Every hill, every bottom and every trail for miles around was being critically searched, and there was hardly a hope for the escape of the brutal young men who had suddenly made such a record of fiendish crimes. For several days the officers trailed them before they began raping. A squad of officers were within about three miles of them when they raped Mrs. Hassen, their first victim, and did not learn anything of it until some hours later when they approached the place and learned of the crime. The search then became

The Muskogee *Phoenix* account of the Buck gang's capture appeared August 15, 1895.

Rufus Buck, Luckey Davis, Maomi July surrendered. Lewis Davis, shot in the calf of one leg, "hid in a ditch during the commotion of the explosion," and escaped. Sam Sampson "fell in the grass and was overlooked." He reached the home of his sister, and "told her he was afraid the citizens were going to kill him. He wanted to get back to the officers and surrender to them for protection; he claimed he preferred standing his chance with the law to getting into another fight like that." His sister hitched up a wagon, concealed him under some quilts in the bed, and started to Okmulgee. "On the road, the officers and citizens with the other prisoners overtook them, and took charge of the frightened Sam."[7]

Angry Indians, whites, and blacks, who had scoured the country with the determination to "work summary punishment" on the Bucks when they were caught, "dropped into line in squads along the road." Among them were friends of Mary Wilson and the Hassan family, and some "begged with tears in their eyes to get the outlaws in their clutches." The deputy marshals and lighthorsemen stood firm, however. They were duty bound to protect the prisoners, inhuman wretches though they were—with their lives, if necessary. The squads of followers quieted somewhat, but continued to "dog" the officers all the way to Okmulgee.[8]

"Some of You Will Die!"

Okmulgee was crowded with people who had come to see the gang in captivity. "Most had suffered in person or through a relative or friend from their crimes, and mobbing was the cry." The local jail was a flimsy affair, and the officers elected to put the prisoners upstairs in the stone capitol building. "A mob, yelling and shooting their guns in the air at once...made a break to get them. The officers ran their team to an open gate in the wall of the capital yard. The prisoners were tied hand and foot, and the officers, in their hurry, threw them out of the wagon. They were too badly scared to see the open gate and tried to climb the wall to escape the crowd. They were rushed into the capitol building and saved."[1]

The Creeks, smarting under repeated accusations of laxity in enforcing and prosecuting their laws, "itched for an opportunity" to dangle the

Bucks at rope's end, and "it looked for a while as if the mob would rescue them from their stronghold." The conservative element "talked to the crowd," however, and the officers promised to keep the prisoners under heavy guard, in handcuffs and shackles, until they could be removed to Fort Smith, where "Judge Parker would execute swift justice." The Creeks "had an abiding faith in Judge Parker in such cases, and the mob sentiment began to subside."[2]

The following day, however, hundreds more people came "from all quarters, of all colors, of all kinds. They were riding mules, horses and ponies, with saddle, bare-backed, blind bridles, rope halters and every kind of quick make-shift. They bore rifles, shotguns, pistols and clubs [and] looked like Falstaff's army....It was an ominous crowd with blood in its eye...and plans were quietly laid to take the prisoners that night."[3]

Irwin telegraphed United States Marshal Crump for reinforcements. Crump replied that reinforcements could not possibly arrive in time. He believed such a large mob would take the prisoners even if they were surrounded by a cordon. He advised transferring them to Muskogee, if possible.

Irwin, Haynes, and Captain Harry "consulted earnestly, while the prisoners quaked in fear." They decided that they could easily steal the Bucks away after dark if not betrayed by the

Thirteen Days of Terror

The Creek Council House (Capitol Building) at Okmulgee—where the Buck prisoners were first taken to protect them from mob action.

clanking of the heavy chains that bound the four together. They told the prisoners if they would pick up their chains and carry them without a sound, they would try to conduct them to safety, and "the wretches, who had so little regard for the lives of others but valued their own so highly," readily agreed. Accordingly, they were slipped away from the capitol building, carrying their chains "a full half mile" without alerting the large groups of men at campfires about the town. They were taken down Okmulgee Creek to the Deep Fork of the Canadian, thence to the little Creek settlement of Hichita by midnight, then to Oktaha on the Katy railroad. There they were hastily loaded in a coach, as arranged by Marshal Rutherford, and landed in the Muskogee jail.[4]

Saturday, August 10, was visitors' day at the federal jail in Muskogee. When the stockade gate was opened, scores of people pushed and scrambled into the yard to await their turn to view the four Bucks. The jailer, identified only as "Rector" in contemporary accounts, admitted them in small groups while the prisoners crouched in the corners of their cell to avoid the onlookers' curious gaze. Only Rufus Buck looked the visitors in the face, steadily and sullenly. The common expression during the day was that the gang should be lynched.

About six o'clock, Benton Callahan, Henry Hassan, and old man Ayers, the father of the girl who had been outraged by the gang and died, arrived in the city. They were merely on their way to Fort Smith to appear as witnesses, but "the presence of these aggrieved parties lent vigor to the mob advocates." It soon became "well understood" that there would be a hanging bee, "to occur that night." By dusk, people from throughout the city were bunched under the arc light on Main Street, "until the street was almost blockaded." Suddenly, the crowd began to move on the jail.[5]

Marshal Rutherford had placed a strong guard in the jail stockade. Rutherford and Chief Deputy McDonald met the mob just before it reached the jail. As the crowd dragged to a halt, the officers began their "speech-making."

McDonald "made an earnest talk which made the mob waver." The government appreciated the indignation which had impelled the people to arise against the Buck gang, he said, but the majesty of the law must be preserved.

Angry men surged forward, but Rutherford stopped them again with these sobering words: "The Jail is stationed with guards, and the prisoners cannot be had without a fight. If you rush the jail, some of you will die!"

Rutherford added, "The life of one of you or one of the guards is worth the whole coop of prisoners." Then he mentioned Judge Parker as "a certain punisher of crime," and the crowd cheered. Men broke away, and began drifting back to town.

By midnight, most of the citizens were in bed. A few who were still out and determined to have a hanging, "stuffed a dummy and hung it on an electric light pole in front of the Patterson Mercantile Company." The next morning, the dummy was "laid to rest," and the Bucks were entrained for Fort Smith without further incident.[6]

When the train arrived at the railroad depot near the bank of the Arkansas Sunday morning, August 11, hundreds of Fort Smith citizens were on hand for "the first opportunity to gaze upon the fiends in human form." As the prisoners came off the train, heavily ironed, with officers in front and behind them, S.W. Harman, author of *Hell on the Border* and a witness to the occasion, could not help saying to himself, "If, by some manner of means those men could be unshackled and all provided with Winchesters, what a scattering there would be!"[7]

Harman continued, "As for the bandits themselves, they appeared wholly unconcerned, though their covert glances took in every face and every detail, and no doubt they longed for the opportunity to make the scattering I have suggested. There was no time lost; the marshals headed for the sidewalk, the crowd separated and with officers leading the way and others bringing up the rear, the procession marched slowly and silently up the avenue…to the gate three blocks away which opened into the old government barracks enclosure...while the morning church bells tolled a requiem to the dead victims....The crowd followed at the officers' heels, continuing until the jail was reached and the creak of the hinges told that another band of outlaws had been placed where they could no longer gloat over human blood."[8]

The missing Lewis Davis had concealed himself until the coast was clear following the Flat Rock fight, then made his way eight miles west to the home of an Indian family he had formerly known, named Richardson. By Saturday evening, the bullet wound in the calf of his leg had become "inflamed and smelling." Richardson managed to get word to Tom Grayson, of the lighthorse.

Monday morning, August 12, Davis "went outside to bathe his wound, taking his Winchester with him. Seeing no one around, he leaned the rifle against the house and proceeded with his ablutions. As he did so, Richardson grabbed the Winchester; at that moment Grayson and Deputy Marshal Irwin "appeared on the scene and made the capture complete." Davis was "not the least excited over his arrest, expressing no fear except from a mob." The officers placed him in a covered wagon, and by traveling at night through the communities where his crimes had been committed, safely reached the railroad at Muskogee. Tuesday night, the outlaw "joined his brother-fiends" in the Fort Smith jail.

Jail physicians announced that his wound was "not very serious...it has never interfered with his locomotion, and bids fair to heal in a short time."[9]

Thirteen days of terror and manhunting had ended. The five Bucks were brought from their cells, in handcuffs and shackles, and photographed as a quintet.

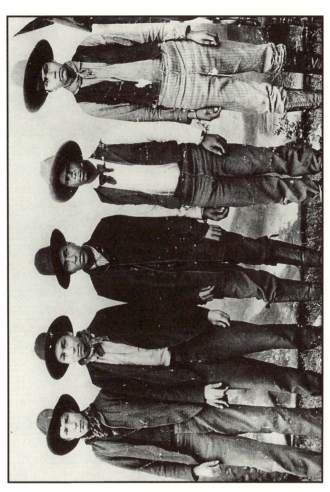

The Rufus Buck gang at the Fort Smith jail: (left to right) Maomi July, Sam Sampson, Rufus Buck, Luckey Davis, and Lewis Davis.

A Flood of Evidence

Assistant United States District Attorney McDonough promptly charged before United States Commissioner Stephen Wheeler that "Rufus Buck, Lewis Davis, Luckey Davis, Sam Sampson and Maomi July, did...on or about the 6th day of August 1895, feloniously, wilfully and maliciously commit an assault upon the person Rosetta Hassan, and her, the said Rosetta Hassan, did forcibly ravish and carnally know, against the peace and dignity of the United States...." The Bucks were committed without bail pending action of the grand jury.[1]

On August 16, the grand jury indicted the Bucks for assault with intent to kill Benton Callahan's cowboy, Sam Houston.[2]

On August 17, Rufus Buck, Lewis Davis, and Luckey Davis were indicted for the murder of Deputy Marshal John Garrett.[3]

Finally, the grand jury indicted all five Bucks

for the rape of Rosetta Hassan.[4] They were arraigned before Judge Parker on Tuesday morning, August 20; they entered pleas of not guilty, and "to allow time for the assembling of witnesses and the flood of evidence," Judge Parker set the trial for Monday, September 23.[5]

The trial began at 8:30 AM. The courtroom was packed with an eager, motley throng "unmindful of the suffocating heat." Many had come for the "mere sake of feeding upon a recital of an awful wickedness...as the buzzard or the vulture is attracted to the polluted carrion whose odor ascends to the heavens"; others to drink in the "loathsome details...and so work themselves to a pitch where they could fully enjoy the punishment [expected] to be dealt for this horrible crime."[6]

Henry Hassan was the first witness examined. He described how the gang rode through his front gate as he was resting beneath the arbor and his wife was preparing fruit nearby; how Rufus Buck had asked for water and the actions of Luckey Davis and the others made him realize he was at the mercy of the gang whose recent depredations had panicked the country; how he had tried to defend his family, but Sam Sampson and Maomi July had seized his weapon; how he had been held under complete subjection by six-shooters and Winchesters while the gang looted his home, forced his wife to prepare a meal for them, and Luckey Davis made her accompany him to the barn; how, afterwards, the gang had marched him and his hired hand two miles away, thrown him in a pool, then, under dire threats of death, made them wrestle and fight each other until both were exhausted; how Rufus Buck had warned him he would be killed should he appear against them; and, finally, how he had hurried home and found his wife hiding in the cornfield, nearly dead from apprehension.

Dick Ryan then took the stand and verified his role in the Hassan drama.

Throughout the testimony, the Bucks "sat unmoved, pretending an inability to understand English." The crowd took in every word with "thrilling interest," and a "murmur of indignation" swept the room when Hassan and Ryan finished speaking. They showed even more interest and indignation when the injured wife and mother took the stand to recite her wrongs.

Rosetta Hassan told much the same story as her husband "in low but tremulous tones showing the strong nervous tension under which she was still laboring." At times, as Assistant District Attorney McDonough propounded questions that brought back with awful vividness the ordeal she had suffered, the woman's breath "came quick, her bosom heaved, the hot blood surged to her temples." She related how she had pleaded with Luckey Davis not to take her away from her babies; how he had threatened to throw them in the creek; how she had complied with his orders only to save the lives of her husband and children; how, at the muzzle of his Winchester, he had marched her to the barn, and...

She paused, head bowed low, and burst into tears. Judge Parker said, kindly, "Just go on and tell everything that occurred there. The law makes it necessary to tell it. It is a very delicate matter, of course, but you will have to tell about it."

McDonough: "Did he tell you what to do?"

"Yes, sir." Her voice was barely audible.

"What did he say?"

"He told me to lie down..." The woman broke completely. Her frame shook and she sobbed like a child.

A "profound silence" swept the courtroom, "broken only by her sobs." Many women in the crowd "gave way to a mighty surge of grief"; there was "scarcely a dry eye" among the jurors; and Judge Parker, who had presided over trials for hundreds of brutal crimes for more than twenty years, removed his spectacles, drew a handkerchief from his pocket, wiped the lenses, and dabbed a suspicious moisture from his lashes.

Several minutes elapsed before Rosetta Hassan regained her composure. After a few gentle words from Judge Parker, she unwillingly described how each of the ruffians had taken their turn, while keeping her husband under the threat of death should he try to rescue her. "The terrible iniquity of the deed came upon Judge Parker with such power that he became livid with rage; it were well for the prisoners that the law prevented him dealing out punishment then and there."

Rosetta Hassan was allowed to step down without cross-examination, the attorneys "standing aside and bowing reverently" as she left the room. William M. Cravens, one of the five attorneys appointed to defend the Bucks, offered nothing against the overwhelming evidence. Turning to Judge Parker, he said simply: "May it please the court and you gentlemen of the jury...I have nothing to say," and resumed his seat. It was the shortest defense plea in the history of the court.

McDonough addressed the jury. "Gentlemen, you have heard the evidence...it is unnecessary to argue the case. The court will give the necessary instruction, and we will expect a verdict of guilty at your hands."

Judge Parker's instructions were "short but impressive." The jury left the room and did not even sit down to ballot. They returned within three minutes with a verdict: "We, the jury, find the defendants Rufus Buck, Lewis Davis, Luckey Davis, Sam Sampson and Maomi July guilty of rape, as charged in the within indictment. [signed] John J. Ferguson, Foreman."[7]

Then occurred another first in the history of the court. Immediately after receiving the verdict, Judge Parker excused the jury, another panel was drawn, a new jury selected, and three of the outlaws, Rufus Buck, Lewis Davis, and Luckey Davis, were put on trial for the murder of Deputy Marshal John Garrett. The case was continued until next day. Rufus Buck tried to prove an alibi—"claimed he was away after recruits"—but a half-dozen witnesses placed him at the scene as the party who fired the fatal shots. This time, the jury was out only twelve minutes before returning with a guilty verdict.[8]

No sentence was passed on the three Bucks in the Garrett case. It was unnecessary. At one o'clock on the afternoon of September 25, a motley crowd again packed the courtroom to suffocation to hear sentence passed upon all five members of the gang for the rape of Rosetta Hassan. It was the second, and the last time in the court's history that so many as five were sentenced at once.

Judge Parker ordered, "Rufus Buck, Lewis Davis, Luckey Davis, Sam Sampson and Maomi July—stand up.

"You have been convicted by a verdict of the jury justly rendered, of the terrible crime of rape. It now becomes the duty of the court to pass sentence upon you, which the law says shall follow a conviction of such crime. Have you anything to say why the sentence of the law should not now be passed in your cases?"

Luckey Davis said, "Yes, sir."

Judge Parker asked, "What is it?"

During the waning years of his tenure on the Fort Smith bench, Parker had been reversed by the United States Supreme Court some thirty times—seldom on the merits of the case, but on merest technicalities—and Luckey Davis said:

"I want my case to go to the Supreme Court."

Judge Parker replied, "I don't blame you a bit," then continued,

> The offense of which you have been convicted is one which shocks all men who are not brutal....It is a violation of the quick sense of honor and the pride of virtue which nature, to render the sex amiable, has implanted in the female heart, and it has been by the law-makers of the United States deemed equal in enormity and wickedness to murder, because the punishment fixed by the same is that which follows the commission of the crime of murder.... The proof shows that each of you first took part in the robbery of the house of Henry Hassan, and afterwards that each of you, in the most revolting and brutal manner, in turn, outraged his wife, Mrs. Rosetta Hassan....The acts so aroused the indignation of your own people, the Creek Indians, that they were almost persuaded to take you from the officers and execute upon you summary vengeance. It was only through respect for the law, and the belief that it would be enforced in this court, that induced them to permit the officers to bring you here.
>
> The enormity and great wickedness of your crime leaves no ground for the extension of sympathy to you....This horrible crime now rests upon your souls. Remove it if you can so the good God of all will extend to you His forgiveness and His mercy....

Judge Isaac Charles Parker, Western District of Arkansas at Fort Smith, sentenced the Buck gang to hang as a quintet.

> Listen now to the sentence of the law which is, that you, Rufus Buck, for the crime of rape, committed by you upon Rosetta Hassan...be deemed, taken and adjudged guilty of rape; and that you be therefor, for the said crime against the laws of the United States, hanged by the neck until you are dead....
>
> May God, whose laws you have broken, and before whose tribunal you must then appear, have mercy on your soul.

Judge Parker then sentenced the remaining four to death and set the time for the quintet's execution between 9:00 AM and 5:00 PM, October 31, 1895.[9]

Luckey Davis sneered at the court's pronouncement; the others showed no sign of emotion and seemed to care nothing for it.

Promised Justice Done

Because Luckey Davis insisted and Rufus Buck contended that, if given an opportunity, he could prove he had not participated in the rape of Rosetta Hassan, Attorney Cravens appealed to the United States Supreme Court. That forced Judge Parker to issue a stay of execution.

But the appeal was in vain. On March, 9, the Supreme Court refused to intervene. "No opinion. Judgments affirmed."[1] The higher court's mandate was received at Fort Smith on Monday, April 27, and on April 28, Judge Parker reset the gang's execution for July 1, 1896.[2] Petitions for pardon on behalf of Sam Sampson and Maomi July were presented to President Grover Cleveland. United States Attorney General Judson Harmon telegraphed United States Marshal Crump, "The President declines to interfere."[3]

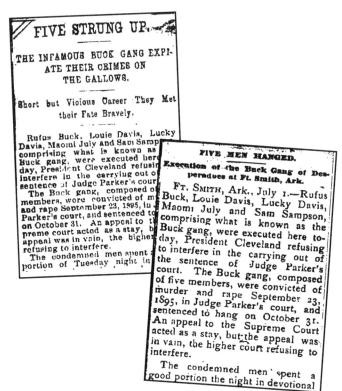

The July 3, 1896, Fort Smith *Elevator* (above) and July 9, 1896, Muskogee *Phoenix* accounts of the Buck gang's execution.

During the last days of June, the condemned men received instruction from Father Pius, of the Roman Catholic Church, and he administered the rite of baptism. The question arose as to the hour that their execution should take place. Luckey Davis wanted to be hanged at 10:30 in the morning, in order that his body could be taken away on the 11:30 train. Rufus Buck objected—this early hour would "inconvenience him by several hours delay" before his body could be on a different train. Finally, they voted four to one that Marshal Crump should set the hour. Crump decided on one o'clock. Luckey Davis then wanted to be hanged by himself, but the marshal explained that he could not alter the court's edict.

The condemned men spent most of the night of June 30 in devotional exercises, singing and praying, retiring at 3:00 AM. "They arose at the usual hour and ate breakfast with the usual relish." At seven minutes past one o'clock the jail door opened.

Rufus Buck came out first, "perfectly calm." The others followed, "equally cool." All were clad in black suits, provided by the government. Buck, Luckey Davis, and July "wore large boutonnieres upon the left lapel of their coats." Many fellow prisoners called "Good-bye, boys," and they responded in "rather low tones." Father Pius accompanied them, and the sisters of Sam Sampson and Luckey Davis followed closely in the march to the gallows.

Marshal Crump had ordered that the execution be conducted in a quiet and orderly manner; that besides prison guards only physicians and reporters would be admitted to the gallows enclosure. Only twenty people were in the jail yard. The citizens of Fort Smith and Indian Territory apparently had become so disgusted with the gang's depredations that few wanted any further sight of them.

As the prisoners entered the gallows enclosure, they glanced up at the hideous paraphernalia, then ascended the steps "without any apparent trepidation." They stood patiently while Marshal Crump read the death warrants. He then asked each in turn. "Have you anything to say?"

"No," one by one replied, until he came to Luckey Davis.

The little Creek-African showed a sudden nervousness by "restless movements and twitchings of his face," as he repeated his former request: "I want to be hanged by myself." Again the request was denied.

"Father Pius uttered a short prayer....This over, the prisoners were motioned to stand on the hinged trap and the dangling nooses were adjusted about their necks." Luckey Davis and Sam Sampson shouted good-byes to their sisters. "The father of Rufus Buck, a big, heavy old man, got into the enclosure and attempted to come up the steps to the platform where his son stood; but he was stupidly drunk, and for that reason was escorted below." The sisters of Sampson and Luckey Davis waited in the enclosure until the black caps were placed in position, then left.

> The trap dropped with its horrible "chug" at 1:25 o'clock. Lewis Davis died in three minutes, his neck broken. The necks of Sam Sampson and Maomi July were also broken, and they died easily....
> Rufus Buck and Luckey Davis were strangled to death. Luckey's body drew up several times before it straightened out. Rufus Buck did not suffer, of course, unconsciousness coming over him as soon as the rope shut off his breath; but it was several minutes before the contortions of his body ceased....
> After the attending physicians had pronounced life extinct, the bodies were cut down and placed in coffins. Four of them were taken to Birnie's undertaking establishment, and from there shipped to their former homes.[4]

There is a family cemetery on the grounds of the old Buck farm near Wealaka. Rufus Buck, however, does not lie there. The family started homeward with his body, but "the weather was warm and they were forced to bury him at Fort Gibson."[5] After the hanging, a photograph of Rufus Buck's mother was found in his cell. On the back, dated July 1, 1896, he had written the following poem and decorated it with a cross and drawing of the Savior:

> i, dremP'T, i, wAs, in, HeAven,
> Among, THe, AngeLs, FAir;

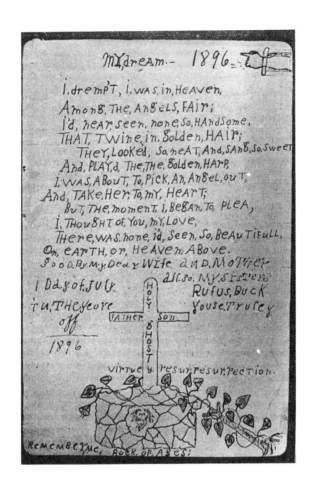

Rufus Buck's "My Dream," written on back of a photograph of his mother, found in his cell after his execution.

> i'd neAr, seen, none, so HAndsome,
> THAT, TWine, in goLden, HAir;
> > THeY, Looked so neAT, and; sAng,
> > so, sweeT
> And, PLAY,d THe THe, goLden, HArp,
> i, wAs ABouT, To, Pick, An, Angel, ouT
> And, TAke, Her, To, mY, HeArT;
> > BuT, THe, momenT, i, BegAn, To,
> > PLeA,
> i, THougHT, oF, You, mY, Love,
> > THere, wAs, none, i'd, seen, so,
> > BeAuTiFuLL,
> On, eArTH, or, HeAven, ABove,
> gooD, By. My. Dear. Wife. anD.
> MoTHer

Some claim this gem reflects the urge that made Rufus Buck a rapist.

Of a certainty, the Indians' faith in the Fort Smith court had been well placed. Out in the Creek Nation, people breathed easy again.

NOTES

Chapter 2

1. Originally *Weakaka*, a Creek word meaning "rising water" or "coming water"—intermittent spring.

2. Angie Debo, *Tulsa: From Creek Town to Oil Capital* (Norman: University of Oklahoma Press, 1943), p. 46; George H. Shirk, *Oklahoma Place Names* (Norman: University of Oklahoma Press, 1965), p. 218; Martha Plummer, "Euchee Visits in Leonard," *Tulsa Tribune*, April 17, 1956.

3. Benton Callahan interview, *Indian-Pioneer History*, Oklahoma Historical Society, Vol. 18, p. 142; Plummer, op. cit.

4. Vinita *Indian Cheiftain*, October 3, 1895; Fort Smith *Elevator*, October 11, 1895.

5. C.H. McKennon, "When the Buck Gang Rode," *True West*, July-August 1976, pp. 25–27.

6. Plummer, op. cit.

7. S.W. Harman, *Hell on the Border* (Fort Smith, Arkansas: The Phoenix Publishing Company, 1898), p. 496.

8. Jerry Rand, "Samuel Morton Rutherford," *Chronicles of Oklahoma*, 30 (Summer 1952), p. 151.

9. Muskogee *Phoenix*, August 1, 1895.

10. Ibid., August 5, 1895.

11. Fort Smith, Arkansas, dispatch, September 23,

Vinita Indian Chieftain, October 3, 1895.

Chapter 3

1. Checotah, Indian Territory dispatch, July 30, Muskogee *Phoenix*, August 1, 1895.
2. Testimony of Newton Armstrong, *United States vs. Rufus Buck, Lewis Davis, and Luckey Davis*, No. 33 (Murder), U.S. Commisioners Court, Fort Smith, Arkansas, filed August 6, 1895.
3. A.J. Kennedy interview, *Indian-Pioneer History*, Oklahoma Historical Society, Vol. 60, pp. 183, 192. (Kennedy was a salesman, buyer, and bookkeeper for the F.B. Severs mercantile chain for six years.)
4. Testimony of Newton Armstrong, op. cit.
5. Muskogee *Phoenix*, October 8, 1895.
6. Ibid., Ardmore *State Herald*, October 8, 1895; Vinita *Indian Chieftain*, October 3, 1895; Harman, op. cit., p. 496.
7. Testimony of Elijah Grayson, *United States vs. Rufus Buck, Lewis Davis and Luckey Davis*, No. 33 (Murder), U.S. Commissioners Court, Fort Smith, Arkansas, filed August 6, 1895.
8. Muskogee *Phoenix*, October 8, 1895.
9. Alec Berryhill interview, *Indian-Pioneer History*, Oklahoma Historical Society, Vol. 14, pp. 478–79.
10. Testimony of Robert Thomas, *United States vs. Rufus Buck, Lewis Davis, and Luckey Davis*, No. 33 (Murder), U.S. Commissioners Court, Fort Smith, Arkansas, filed August 6, 1895.
11. Muskogee *Phoenix*, September 5, 1895.
12. Ibid., August 8, 1895.

Chapter 4

1. Muskogee *Phoenix*, August 8, 1895; Ardmore *State*

Herald, August 22, 1895; *Oklahoma Daily Times -Journal*, August 24, 1895.

2. Muskogee *Phoenix*, August 8, 1895; Harman, op. cit., p. 497.

3. Benton Callahan interview, *Indian-Pioneer History*, Oklahoma Historical Society, Vol. 18, p. 141.

4. Ibid., pp. 141–42.

5. Muskogee *Phoenix*, August 8, 1895.

6. Checotah, Indian Territory, dispatch, August 21, Muskogee *Phoenix*, August 22, 1895. (Harman, in *Hell on the Border*, p. 497, states erroneously, "Houston afterwards died of his wounds.")

7. Fort Smith *Elevator*, July 3, 1896; Muskogee *Phoenix*, July 9, 1896; Harman, op. cit., p. 497.

8. Mrs. Dollie Garretson to Bill Hoge, "Oologah Oozings," Tulsa *Sunday World*, April 22, 1962.

9. Fort Smith *Elevator*, July 3, 1896; Muskogee *Phoenix*, July 9, 1896; Harman, op. cit., p. 496.

10. William Frank Jones interview, *Indian-Pioneer History*, Oklahoma Historical Society, Vol. 149, p. 24; Wm. F. Jones, *The Experiences of a Deputy U.S. Marshal of the Indian Territory* (privately printed in Tulsa, Oklahoma, April 19, 1937).

11. Muskogee *Phoenix*, August 8, 1895. (Name of victim not given.)

12. Ibid.

13. Ibid.

14. *United States vs. Rufus Buck, Lewis Davis, and Luckey Davis*, No. 33, op. cit.

15. *United States vs. Rufus Buck, Lewis Davis and Luckey Davis*, No. 455 (Capias), U.S. Commissioners Court, Fort Smith, Arkansas, filed August 6, 1895.

16 *United States vs. Rufus Buck, Lewis Davis, Luckey Davis, Sam Sampson, and Maomi July*, No. 336 (Assault with Intent to Kill), U.S. Commissioners Court, Fort Smith, Arkanasas, filed August 6, 1895.

17. Muskogee *Phoenix*, August 8, 1895.

Chapter 5

1. Details of the attack on the Hassan Family from the testimony of Henry Hassan, Rosetta Hassan, and Dick Ryan, *United States vs. Rufus Buck, Lewis Davis, Luckey Davis, Sam Sampson and Maomi July*, No. 144 (Rape), U.S. District Court, Fort Smith, Arkansas, filed August 20, 1895.

See also Ardmore *State Herald*, August 22, 1895; *Oklahoma Daily Times-Journal*, August 24, 1895; Vinita *Indian Chieftain*, October 3, 1895; Fort Smith *Elevator*, July 3, 1896; Muskogee *Phoenix*, July 6–9, 1896; Harman, op cit., pp. 496–97, 505–10.

Chapter 6

1. Muskogee *Phoenix*, August 8 and 15, 1895.
2. J.I. Belford interview, C.H. McKennon, "When the Buck Gang Rode," op. cit.
3. Muskogee *Phoenix*, August 15, 1895; Fort Smith *Elevator*, July 3, 1896; Alec Berryhill interview, op. cit.
4. Muskogee *Phoenix*, August 15, 1895; Ardmore *State Herald*, August 22, 1895; Harman, op. cit., pp. 497–98.
5. Ardmore *State Herald*, September 12, 1895; Vinita *Indian Chieftain*, September 26, 1895.
6. Muskogee *Phoenix*, August 15, 1895; Harman, op. cit., p. 500.
7. Muskogee *Phoenix*, August 15, 1895.
8. Ibid., Ardmore *State Herald*, August 22, 1895; *Oklahoma Daily Times-Journal*, August 24, 1895.

Chapter 7

1. Muskogee *Phoenix*, August 15, 1895.

2. Ibid.; Harman, op. cit., p. 501.

3. Muskogee *Phoenix*, August 15, 1895; Ardmore *State Herald*, August 22, 1895.

4. Muskogee *Phoenix*, August 15, 1895; Ardmore *State Herald*, August 22, 1895; Harman, op. cit., p. 502; William F. Jones, *The Experience of a Deputy U.S. Marshal*, op. cit., p. 4.

5. Muskogee *Phoenix*, August 15, 1895; Ardmore *State Herald*, August 22, 1895; *Oklahoma Daily Times-Journal*, August 24, 1895; Fort Smith *Elevator*, August 30, 1895.

6. Ibid.

7. Harman, op. cit., p. 503.

8. Ibid.

9. Muskogee *Phoenix*, August 15, 1895; *Daily Oklahoman*, September 3, 1895; Ardmore *State Herald*, September 12, 1895.

Chapter 8

1. *United States vs. Rufus Buck, Lewis Davis, Luckey Davis, Sam Sampson and Maomi July*, No. —, (Rape) U.S. Commissioners Court, Fort Smith, Arkansas, filed August 13, 1895.

2. *United States vs. Rufus Buck, Lewis Davis, Luckey Davis, Sam Sampson and Maomi July*, No. 336 (Grand Jury Indictment—Assault with Intent to Kill), U.S. District Court, Fort Smith, Arkanasas, filed August 16, 1895.

3. *United States vs. Rufus Buck, Lewis Davis and Luckey Davis*, No. 158 (Grand jury indictment—Murder), U.S. District Court, Fort Smith, Arkansas, filed August 17, 1895.

4. *United States vs. Rufus Buck, Lewis Davis, Luckey Davis, Sam Sampson and Maomi July*, No. 144 (Grand jury joint indictment—Rape), U.S. District Court, Fort Smith, Arkansas, filed August 20, 1895.

5. Muskogee *Phoenix*, August 22, 1895; Harman, op.

cit., p. 504.

6. Harman, op. cit., p. 505.

7. Testimony and proceedings, *United States vs. Rufus Buck, Lewis Davis, Luckey Davis, Sam Sampson and Maomi July*, No. 144 (Rape), U.S. District Court, Fort Smith, Arkansas, September 23, 1895; Muskogee *Phoenix*, September 26, 1895; Vinita *Indian Chieftain*, October 3, 1895; Harman, op. cit., pp. 505–10.

8. Testimony and proceedings, *United States vs. Rufus Buck, Lewis Davis and Luckey Davis*, No. 158 (Murder), U.S. District Court, Fort Smith, Arkansas, September 23–24, 1895; Muskogee *Phoenix*, September 26, 1895; Harman, op. cit., p. 511.

9. *United States vs. Rufus Buck, Lewis Davis, Luckey Davis, Sam Sampson and Maomi July*, No. 144 (Sentence of the Court—Rape), U.S. District Court, Fort Smith, Arkansas, September 25, 1895.

Chapter 9

1. *Buck et al. vs. United States*, No. 792, U.S. Supreme Court Mandate, March 9, 1896; *Buck et al. vs. United States*, 163 U.S. 678.

2. Vinita *Indian Chieftain*, April 30, 1896.

3. Ibid., June 25, 1896.

4. Fort Smith *Elevator*, July 3, 1896; Muskogee *Phoenix*, July 9, 1896.

5. Plummer, op. cit.

SOURCES

Documents

Buck et al. vs. United States, No. 792, U.S. Supreme Court Mandate, March 9, 1896, 163 U.S. 678.

United States vs. Rufus Buck, Lewis Davis and Luckey Davis, No. 33 (Murder), U.S. Commissioners Court, Fort Smith, Arkansas, filed August 6, 1895.

United States vs. Rufus Buck, Lewis Davis and Luckey Davis, No. 455 (Capias), U.S. Commissioners Court, Fort Smith, Arkanasas, filed August 6, 1895.

United States vs. Rufus Buck, Lewis Davis and Luckey Davis, No. 158 (Grand jury indictment—Murder), U.S. District Court, Fort Smith, Arkansas, filed August 27, 1895.

United States vs. Rufus Buck, Lewis Davis and Luckey Davis, No. 158 (Testimony and proceedings—Murder), U.S. District Court, Fort Smith, Arkansas, September 23–24, 1895.

United States vs. Rufus Buck, Lewis Davis, Luckey Davis, Sam Sampson and Maomi July, No. 336 (Grand jury indictment—Assault with Intent to Kill), U.S. Commissioners Court, Fort Smith, Arkansas, filed August 6, 1895.

United States vs. Rufus Buck, Lewis Davis, Luckey Davis, Sam Sampson and Maomi July, No. — (Rape), U.S. Commissioners Court, Fort Smith, Arkansas, filed August 13, 1895.

United States vs. Rufus Buck, Lewis Davis, Luckey Davis, Sam Sampson and Maomi July, No. 336 (Grand jury indictment—Assault with Intent to Kill), U.S. District Court, Fort Smith, Arkansas, filed August 16, 1895.

United States vs. Rufus Buck, Lewis Davis, Luckey Davis, Sam Sampson and Maomi July, No. 144 (Rape), U.S. District Court, Fort Smith, Arkansas, filed August 20, 1895.

United States vs. Rufus Buck, Lewis Davis, Luckey Davis, Sam Sampson and Maomi July, No. 144 (Grand jury joint indictment—Rape), U.S. District Court, Fort Smith, Arkansas, filed August 20, 1895.

United States vs. Rufus Buck, Lewis Davis, Luckey Davis, Sam Sampson and Maomi July, No. 144 (Testimony and proceedings—Rape), U.S. District Court, Fort Smith, Arkansas, September 23, 1895.

United States vs. Rufus Buck, Lewis Davis, Luckey Davis, Sam Sampson and Maomi July, No. 144 (Sentence of the court—Rape), U.S. District Court, Fort Smith, Arkansas, September 25, 1895.

Newspapers

Ardmore *State Herald,* August 22, 1895; September 12, 1895; October 3 and 8, 1895.

Daily Oklahoman, September 3 and 8, 1895.

Fort Smith *Elevator*, August 30, 1895; July 3, 1896.

Muskogee *Phoenix*, August 1, 5, 8, 15, and 22, 1895; September 5 and 26, 1895; October 8, 1895; November 28, 1895; July 6 and 9, 1896.

Oklahoma Daily Times-Journal, August 24, 1895; July 2, 1896.

Vinita *Indian Chieftain*, September 26, 1895; October 3, 1895; April 30, 1896; June 25, 1896; July 2, 1896.

Interviews

In *Indian-Pioneer History,* Oklahoma Historical Society,

Archives and Manuscript Division, Volumes 1–112.
   Callahan, Benton. Vol. 18, 141, 142.
   Kennedy, A.J. Vol. 60, 183, 192.
   Berryhill, Alec. Vol. 14, 478-479.
   Jones, William Frank. Vol. 24, 149.

Books and Pamphlets

Benedict, John D. *History of Muskogee and Northeastern Oklahoma* (II). Chicago: S.J. Clarke, 1922.

Buchanan, James Shannon and Edward Everett Dale. *A History of Oklahoma*. Evanston, Illinois: Row, Peterson, and Company, 1939.

Croy, Homer. *He Hanged Them High*. New York: Duell, Sloan and Pearce; and Boston: Little, Brown, and Company, 1952.

Debo, Angie. *The Road to Disappearance*. Norman: University of Oklahoma Press, 1941.

_____. *Tulsa: From Creek Town to Oil Capital*. Norman: University of Oklahoma Press, 1943.

Drago, Harry Sinclair. *Outlaws on Horseback*. New York: Dodd, Mead and Company, 1964.

Dunn, J.E. *Indian Territory, A Precommonwealth*. Indianapolis, Indiana: American Printing Company, 1904.

Emery, J. Gladstone. *Court of the Damned*. New York: Comet Press Books, 1959.

Harman, S.W. *Hell on the Border*. Fort Smith, Arkansas: Phoenix Publishing Company, 1898.

Harrington, Fred Harvey. *Hanging Judge*. Caldwell, Idaho: The Caxton Printers, Ltd., 1951.

Jones, Wm. F. *The Experience of a Deputy U.S. Marshal of the Indian Territory*. Tulsa, Oklahoma: Privately printed, 1937.

McKennon, C.H. *Iron Men*. Garden City, New York: Doubleday & Company, Inc., 1967.

Shirk, George H. *Oklahoma Place Names*. Norman: University of Oklahoma Press, 1965.

Shirley, Glenn. *Law West of Fort Smith*. New York: Henry Holt & Company, 1957.

West, C.W. *Outlaws and Peace Officers of Indian Territory*. Muskogee, Oklahoma: Muskogee Printing Company, 1987.

_____. *Persons and Places in Indian Territory*. Muskogee, Oklahoma: Muskogee Printing Company, 1974.

Articles

"Judge Parker's Justice." *The Oklahoma Cowman*, August 1968.

Daily, Harry P. "Judge Isaac C. Parker." *Chronicles of Oklahoma*, Vol. XI, No. 1 (March 1933).

Garretson, Mrs. Dollie. "Oologah Oozings." *Tulsa Sunday World*, April 22, 1962.

Glynn, Dean. "The Buck Gang's 13 Days of Terror." *Westerner*, March-April 1969. Reprinted in September-October 1973.

Harrison, John H. "70,000 Square Miles of Violence." *Frontier West*, April 1973.

McKennon, C.H. "When the Buck Gang Rode." *True West*, July-August 1976.

Meyers, Olevia E. "Rufus Buck's 13 Days of Hell." *Real West*, July 1965.

Plummer, Martha. "Euchee Chief Visits in Leonard." *Tulsa Tribune*, April 17, 1956.

Rand, Jerry. "Samuel Morton Rutherford." *Chronicles of Oklahoma*, Vol. XXX, No. 2 (Summer 1952).

Shanks, Davis C. "Indian Territory Incidents." *Frontier Times*, July 1929.

INDEX

Arbekochee (Arbeka), Indian Territory: 6, 39
Ardmore, Indian Territory: 14
Arkansas River: 6, 8, 10, 11, 52
Armstrong, Newton: 30
Atoka, Indian Territory: 14
Ayers (white farmer): 23, 50
Ayers girl: 23-24, 31

Beggs, Oklahoma: 12
Belford, J.I.: 11–13, 38
Belford, N.R. "Newt": 11–13, 32, 38-39
Bell, Dr. (Okmulgee physician): 22
Berryhill, Alec: 21-22
Berryhill, Stanford: 42
Berryhill, Thomas: 42
Berryhill, William: 42
Berryhill Creek: 24
"Big Nellie": 20–21
Birnie (undertaker): 69
Borden (sales agent): 19
Brown, George: 41
Brown, Samuel W.: 10, 13
Brown, W.S.: 13
Buck, John: 9, 16, 21, 68-69
Buck, Rufus: 9–11, 13–14, 16–18, 20–24, 26-27, 29–30, 33–36, 38-39, 41, 42-44, 46, 48, 50, 56–58, 60–61, 64–65, 67, 69, 71
Byers & Leven: 18–19

Callahan, Benton: 8-9, 11, 24–25, 50, 56
Callahan, S.P.: 11, 24
Chambers, Gus: 26
Canadian River: 6
Checotah, Indian Territory: 18-20, 25, 29, 38
Cherokee Indians: 5–6
Cherokee Nation: 8, 11, 14
Childers, Daniel "Goob": 10-11
Cleveland, President Grover: 65
Cook, Bill: 13
Coweta district (Creek Nation): 3, 8
Cravens, William M.: 60, 65
Creek Indians: 4–5, 7, 9, 47–48, 62
Creek Nation: 11, 29–30, 33, 71
Crump, George J.: 30, 48, 65, 67–68

Davis, Dr. (Checotah physician): 25

Davis, Lewis: 11–13, 16, 20–21, 23, 29–30, 34–35, 46, 53, 56, 60–61, 65, 69
Davis, Luckey: 11–13, 16, 20–21, 23, 27, 29–30, 33–35, 46, 56–58, 60–62, 64, 65, 67–69
Dawes Severalty Act: 9
Deep Fork district (Creek Nation): 3
Deep Fork of the Canadian: 3, 50
Duck Creek: 10, 26

Euchee Indians: 9
Eufaula, Indian Territory: 7
Eufala district (Creek Nation): 3, 7

Father Pius: 67–68
Ferguson, John J.: 60
Five Civilized Tribes: 9
"Flat Rock": 41–42, 44, 53
Flatrock Creek: 41
Fort Gibson, Indian Territory: 69
Fort Smith, Arkansas: 4, 13–14, 16, 29, 42, 48, 51–52, 53, 65, 68, 71

Garretson, Dollie: 26
Garrett, John: 21-22, 30, 56, 61
George, Jensie: 12

Goldsby, Crawford "Cherokee Bill": 13-14
Gossett, John: 42
Grave Creek: 8
Grayson, Elijah: 21, 30
Grayson, Tom: 41, 53

Half Moon ranch: 29
Harman, S.W.: 43, 52
Harmon, Judson: 65
Harry, Edmund: 38, 41–42, 44, 48
Hassan, Henry: 31–38, 46, 50, 57, 61, 62
Hassan, Rosetta: 32–38, 46, 56–61, 62, 64, 65
Haynes, Samuel: 30, 38, 41, 48
Hell on the Border: 43-44, 52
Hines, W.H.: 42
Hichita, Indian Territory: 50
House of Kings: 3–4
House of Warriors: 3–4
Houston, Sam (cowboy): 24–25, 30, 56

Indian Territory: 29, 68
Intercourse Law: 6
Irwin, N.B.: 30, 38, 41, 48, 53

Jones, Jesse H.: 25, 30, 38
Jones, William Frank: 25–27
July, Maomi: 16, 23, 24,

25, 30, 34–35, 46, 56–57, 60–61, 65, 67, 69

Keating, Lawrence: 14
Knobble (merchant): 39, 42

Lenapah, Indian Territory: 14
Leonard, Oklahoma: 10

McAlester, Indian Territory: 14
McDermott, Indian Territory: 39
McDonald (chief deputy marshal): 51
McDonough, John B. "Buck": 29, 43, 56, 58–60
McMullen, J.A.: 42
Malcolm, Freddie: 26
Meagher, T.F.: 8
Minter, J.H.: 42
Minter, M.L.: 8
Missouri, Kansas and Texas (Katy) railroad: 18, 50
Moore, Mark: 16, 21
Muskogee, Indian Territory: 7–8, 14, 20, 30, 48, 50-51, 53
Muskogee district (Creek Nation): 3, 7–8
Muskogee *Phoenix*: 14, 16, 24, 29–30

Natura, Indian Territory: 23
Norburg, Louis: 6
Norburg & Company: 39
North Fork of the Canadian: 39

Oklahoma Territory: 4
Okmulgee, Indian Territory: 3, 9, 11, 16, 18, 20-22, 24, 29, 39, 41, 46, 47
Okmulgee Creek: 50
Okmulgee district (Creek Nation): 3, 10
Oktaha, Indian Territory: 50
Orcutt, A.D.: 11–12
Orcutt, Adaline: 11–12
Orcutt, Indian Territory: 12, 31–32, 38

Parkinson (Indian Trader): 20–22
Parker, Isaac Charles: 14, 42–43, 48, 51, 57, 59–62, 64–65
Patterson Mercantile Company: 52
Pawnee reservation: 4
Perry, Mitchell: 18-19
Pigeon, Dave: 22
Pigeon, Jesse: 22
Preston, Oklahoma: 41
Rector (Muskogee jailer): 50
Richardson (Indian): 53
Rutherford, Samuel

Morton: 14, 30–31, 50, 51
Ryan, Dick: 32, 36–37, 58

Sac and Fox reservation: 4
Sampson, Sam: 16, 23, 30, 34, 35, 46, 56–57, 60–61, 65, 67–69
Sapulpa, Indian Territory: 26
Seminole Nation: 7–8, 9, 23
Severs, F.B.: 8, 20
Shafey, Jim: 24
Shannon, George: 8
Shannon and Company: 8
"Shansey" (Indian): 41, 44
Sloan, C.G.: 42, 44
Snake Creek: 10, 17, 31–32, 35-36
Spaulding, H.B.: 8
Spaulding & Company: 18–19
Stanford (posseman): 42
Stewart, Dr. (Checotah physician): 25

Thomas (posseman): 42
Thomas, Robert: 22, 30
Tiger, Monty: 29
Tobler, Sandy: 41
Tulsa, Indian Territory: 10, 11, 12
Tulsey (Cussetah tribal town): 16
Turner, H.G.: 18–19, 20
Tuskegee hills: 39

U-Bar ranch: 9, 11, 24–25

Walker, Harry: 42
Wealaka, Indian Territory: 13, 26, 69
Wealaka Mission: 10–11, 24
West, Dr. (Checotah physician): 20
Western District of Arkansas: 29
Wheeler, Stephen: 29–30, 56
Wilson, Charles: 26–27
Wilson, Mary: 26-27, 46
Wilson, Zeke: 16, 18, 22
Wisdom, Dew M. (Indian agent): 7
Wewoka district (Creek Nation): 3, 7

ABOUT THE AUTHOR

Glenn Shirley is a widely recognized authority on the Old West, especially outlaws and lawmen of Indian Territory and Oklahoma. He has authored more than twenty books, including the definitive account of "Hanging Judge" Isaac Parker's court and biographies of Heck Thomas, Bill Tilghman, Belle Starr, and Henry Starr.

Mr. Shirley's previous Barbed Wire Press titles are *Purple Sage: The Exploits, Adventures, and Writings of Patrick Sylvester McGeeney, Gunfight at Ingall: Death of an Outlaw Town, They Outrobbed Them All: The Rise and Fall of the Vicous Martins*, and *Marauders of the Indian Nations: The BIll Cook Gang and Cherokee Bill.*